FIRST
BIOGRAPHIES

Sacagawea

Published by Raintree Steck-Vaughn Publishers, an imprint of Steck-Vaughn Company

Retold for young readers by Edith Vann
Editor: Pam Wells
Project Manager: Julie Klaus
Electronic Production: Scott Melcer

Library of Congress Cataloging-in-Publication Data

Gleiter, Jan, 1947-
    Sacagawea / by Jan Gleiter and Kathleen Thompson; [retold for young readers by Edith Vann]; illustrated by Yoshi Miyake.
      p.   cm. — (First biographies)
    ISBN 0-8114-8453-X
    1. Sacagawea, 1786-1884 — Juvenile literature.   2. Shoshoni women — Biography — Juvenile literature.   3. Lewis and Clark Expedition (1804-1806) — Juvenile literature.   I. Thompson, Kathleen.   II. Vann, Edith.   III. Miyake, Yoshi.   IV. Title.   V. Series.
F592.7.S123G55   1995
970.004'97 — dc20   94-43269
[B]   CIP   AC

Printed and bound in the United States
1 2 3 4 5 6 7 8 9 0 W 99 98 97 96 95

FIRST
BIOGRAPHIES
Sacagawea

Jan Gleiter and Kathleen Thompson
Illustrated by Yoshi Miyake

RSVP
RAINTREE
STECK-VAUGHN
PUBLISHERS
The Steck-Vaughn Company

Austin, Texas

It was a hot summer morning in 1805. Two women and a little girl were walking through a valley. They were Shoshone Indians. Suddenly they saw a group of strange men. They had pale skin and hair on their faces. The Shoshone women were very frightened.

The men came closer. One reached into his pack. The little girl closed her eyes in fear. She opened her eyes. The man held a string of beads for her. Then he leaned down. He rubbed red paint on her cheeks. She knew what that meant. It was a Shoshone sign for peace.

The women got beads, too. Their cheeks were painted red. The Shoshones led the men to their camp. On the way, they met sixty Shoshone warriors on horses. The warriors saw the signs of peace and gifts. They welcomed the explorers.

The leader of the strangers was Meriwether Lewis. His group needed help to go on exploring. They could not speak the Shoshone language. And the Shoshones could not speak their language, English. Lewis knew that soon the rest of his group would arrive. William Clark led the other group. With Clark was a young woman who could speak the Shoshone language. Her name was Sacagawea.

Lewis and the Shoshones could use only sign language. It was not easy to talk this way. Lewis told them that he and his men were friendly. But he could not explain what they were doing there. He could not explain why their trip was so important.

Imagine what the United States was like in 1805. In the East there were farms and towns and cities. But no one knew what the land was like west of the Mississippi River. No one knew who lived there.

Oregon Country

Louisiana Territory

Mexico

Different Indian tribes lived west of the Mississippi. Each tribe knew the land they lived in. And they knew nearby land but not the rest.

This wild land had just been bought from France in 1803. It was called the Louisiana Territory. This was the land between the Mississippi River and the Rocky Mountains.

United Stateles

Florida

Map of North America 1803

11

At that time, Thomas Jefferson was the President of the United States. He wanted to know what the Louisiana Territory was like. He didn't know about its rivers or mountains. He didn't know what the plants, animals, or people were like. Thomas Jefferson sent Meriwether Lewis and William Clark to find out.

Lewis and Clark bought boats, medicine, tools, and food. They bought gifts for the Indians. Paper and ink were for maps and reports. With forty-three others, Lewis and Clark began their trip. They left from St. Louis, Missouri, on May 14, 1804.

By November the explorers were in what is now North Dakota. There they stopped for the winter. Later they would go to the Rocky Mountains. President Jefferson wanted them to go all the way to the Pacific Ocean. To do that, they would have to cross the mountains. They could not cross without horses.

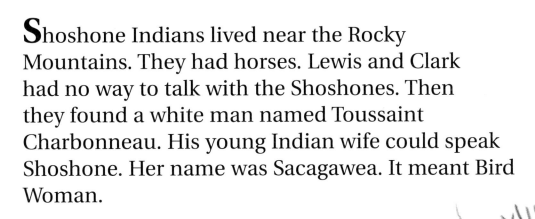

Shoshone Indians lived near the Rocky Mountains. They had horses. Lewis and Clark had no way to talk with the Shoshones. Then they found a white man named Toussaint Charbonneau. His young Indian wife could speak Shoshone. Her name was Sacagawea. It meant Bird Woman.

Neither Lewis nor Clark liked Charbonneau. But they agreed to give him a job if he would bring Sacagawea.

The explorers set out in the spring. Charbonneau and Sacagawea went along, with their baby, Jean Baptiste Charbonneau.

Sacagawea was only about seventeen years old. But she seemed older. Perhaps it was because her life as a child had been cut short.

Sacagawea was a Shoshone Indian. She was born in what we call Idaho. When she was about eleven, her people were attacked by Hidatsa Indians. Sacagawea was caught by an enemy warrior on horseback. She was taken to live with the Hidatsas. Later Charbonneau won her in a bet with the Hidatsa chief. Sacagawea became his wife.

Now she was on her way home. She would see where she had lived.

By late July the explorers were in what we call western Montana. Sacagawea knew the land. She told Lewis and Clark they were near her people, the Shoshones.

This group traveled in boats. But Lewis and a few others went ahead on foot. Lewis was trying to find the Shoshones.

A few days later Clark was walking behind Sacagawea. She began to dance with joy. She had seen Lewis and the Shoshones.

Sacagawea was happy to find several of her friends. One young woman had also been taken away. Later she escaped from the Hidatsas and came home. Now they were together again.

At last the explorers and the Shoshones talked. They sat in a circle and passed a peace pipe. Smoking the pipe was a sign of being friends. The Shoshones took off their moccasins. Lewis and Clark took off their boots. This meant that any promise made would be kept. Whoever broke a promise would walk with bare feet forever.

Sacagawea sat down with the men. Then she saw the chief. To Lewis and Clark's surprise, she ran to him. She threw her arms around him. The chief was her brother!

Sacagawea helped the explorers explain their trip. There was no Shoshone word for "president." So she called Thomas Jefferson "the Great Father." The Shoshones did not know our name for the Pacific Ocean. She said they must go all the way to the Big Water.

The Shoshones agreed to sell horses to Lewis and Clark. They promised guides to show the way across the Rocky Mountains.

Soon Lewis and Clark had to go on. Sacagawea went with them. Her most important job was over. Still there were many ways she could help.

She could show the best way through land she knew. She could find roots and berries safe to eat.

Sacagawea was a great help in another way. Many Indians lived between the Rockies and the Pacific. Few had ever seen white people. Without her, the group might often have been in danger. Seeing Sacagawea and her baby calmed the Indians. They could tell that the explorers came in peace.

The trip was long and hard. But Sacagawea never gave up. She traveled all the way to the Pacific Ocean. Then she went back across the Rocky Mountains.

Once she walked fourteen days with her baby on her back. She was wet and cold and hungry. Today people make that trip by car in three hours.

The Lewis and Clark adventure was a great success. The explorers returned safely to St. Louis in September of 1806. Much had been learned about the western lands. Settlers moved to the West. Towns grew. Railroads were built where there had been only Indian paths.

Without Sacagawea, Lewis and Clark might not have been able to do this. She had helped make a great difference in America. Sacagawea had done what was needed. It was a hard job, and she had done it well.

Key Dates

1784? Born near Lehmi, Idaho, a member of the Shoshone nation.

1800 Captured by the Hidatsa.

1804 Became wife to Toussaint Charbonneau.

1805 Gave birth to Jean Baptiste Charbonneau on February 11. Became a guide and interpreter for the Lewis and Clark expedition.

Note: We do not know the dates of Sacagawea's birth and death. She was probably born between 1784 and 1787. A mountain pass, a peak, and a river are all named for her. There are memorials to her at Bismarck, North Dakota; Three Forks, Montana; Portland, Oregon; and near Dillon, Montana.